Permanent

Vacation

A Handbook of Golden Age Proportions

Gabriel Othon

ISBN-13: 978-1475250800

ISBN-10: 1475250800

Library of Congress Control Number: **2016908026**

Createspace Independent Publishing Platform

These pages are for the cause.

CONTENTS

ACKNOWLEDGMENTS

Eternal thanks to my vigilant family. Their patience and support meant everything. A big thanks to my college professors for opening my eyes to the world.

1

GRACE

The question is, what can you afford? The bottom line is, what do you want the most? Vice is where civilization pulls the leash on us. Image is public trust. What you do reflects on your associates. Even friends will draw the line on you. It is now when you will appreciate good investments made earlier. A good policy to stick with is to always leave a vice better than you found it. You are your main investor, after all.

Lust is the greatest obstacle to modern family values. It is a biological jack-in-the-box and a finite encounter with prevailing fertility gods. Monogamous relationships are always the answer home wreckers need. Backsliding indiscretions, only partially satisfying, are a last resort. Overriding impulses cannot be satiated for apparent reasons. Cozy nooks serve in a pinch. World-spinning swivels pin daredevils against walls while companions urge them to get a room. Also, depravity falls out of closets, sexually transmitted diseases happen, and three dimensional mementos have hungry mouths to feed.

Gluttony is the rock bottom answer to instant gratification. Food never says no and is oh so satisfying. Feast like a king or binge on comfort food; give in to the goodness. Diets are for wimps, flavor is everything, and cuisine is global. Refine the palate and season taste; menus are select. Lace spices are rare, restricted as controlled substances in bulk markets. The heart attack is sudden, clothes no longer flatter, and the obesity can be seen in the mirror. Also, food may disagree with you.

Greed is the slipperiest slope on the block. With fortune comes power, fame, and opportunity. It is here where civilization taps out and business steps up. All cards are on the table, surprise is gone, and the cash influx is automatic. All ledgers are detailed; revenuers are thorough; accounts are in the tropics. Hard times spiral out of control. Life insurance kills, franchises eclipse the natives, and the poor guy learns cooperation the hard way.

Sloth is the domain of the aimless. Diversions are no obstacle to lifestyle for the ambivalent individual. Video games are equally as productive as music mixes. Akin to leisure, activity is subordinate, and mornings are slept away. There is heavy drinking to do, with television on demand and maybe time to explore the web. Interventions are pending, fitness is a shambles, hygiene is a bother, and mental health is questioned by acquaintances.

Wrath is the most disruptive of all the vices. Refugees flee before it, soundtracks make it an entertainer, and its minions are heaped with glory. Bloody hands marinate imaginations, desensitized morality brings out voyeurs, and local doppelgängers push retreating limits. Suddenly, dominance is paramount, violent offenders are registered by law enforcement, and authorities are on alert. Blind rage perseveres, outbursts are discounted, and reckonings still loom.

Envy is the berserker. Born in the taboo, it is forever out of the blue. Pleasant fantasies consume the hours, backstabbing looks good, and swashbuckling is a slash away. Enriching returns on plunder look promising; prospects look promising; yesterday promised. Opportunities disintegrate at a touch, hard feelings spoil bonds, and gossip flies high in any event.

Pride is genuine satisfaction. It is like oxygen, but can be shared or withheld as seen fit. It is a staple of health, a natural high, and a welcome friend. It is a fickle master who is missed when gone and can be a problem child. Prone to martyrdom, pride is vulnerable to blindside betrayal and hot on ashes for dinner.

Beyond the requested goal of gracious hosts to not disappoint them in public, there is the opportunity to impress. For thousands of years, humanity has revered and preserved crowd pleasers as virtues to live by. Also numbering seven like vice, the first four are known as the cardinal (from the Latin 'cardo' meaning 'hinge') virtues, while the last three were adapted from church origins.

Prudence, once said to be the perfect virtue, encompassing all the others, is seen more simply as savvy today. It is all-in-one dominion; it is the cavalry on the plains. Commended instead of prosecuted, advanced instead of forgotten, it is recognized as potential and entrusted with real power. Prudence is reliable under the gun, vigilant in the darkness, and poised in the spotlight. It is also always on call; it suffers for the cause and sacrifices for the greater good.

Fortitude is another way of saying courage. It exists in a vacuum, beyond which lies family, friends, neighbors, and customers. Pertinent gambles are in hand, crucibles are underfoot, and destiny is on the table. The flip side of attitude sees a baptism of fire—the game in the proverbial bush, and later, plans on the line. Success means a better life, failure costs profoundly, and stunted byes haunt coward reputation and survivor mettle.

Temperance, or restraint, is a game of patience. It is crucial to fill the void with worthy diversion and activities when swearing off unseemly behavior forever. Temperance is where spiritual journeys begin, embarrassing behavior ends, and dust covers the toys. Line of sight is the meaning of life, diet and exercise are the way of life, and legacies are the way to eternal life. Sadly, after due consideration, you are going to miss the party, close friends are going to miss you, but loved ones will know you think of them.

Justice is the remedy civilization concocted to address criminal injuries. Sacrifice is a very personal matter that is meant to be dispensed at the discretion of the individual. Forgiveness is prudent, revenge is savage, but injustice is uncivilized. Justice is closure for open matters and a stitch in time for due consideration, but it is not a source for personal satisfaction. It separates man from beast. Its jigsaw path cuts to the bone. Its bold strokes sooth alarming statistical charts. Foundations are founded, monuments are commissioned, and hard memorials are best slept on, for tormented souls.

Faith is the leap of life, not only with a partner but for a supreme being. It is an alley-oop that delights and amazes. Faith is a leap into open arms from the jaws of death and despair, or it is a tandem act of synergy. When redeemed it is galvanized; when shaken it is tenuous; when shot it is shunned. Honest introspection of faith foretells the heart, open displays of faith bleed the heart, consummation of faith warms the heart, and betrayal of faith ices it.

Hope is the swivel that lives turn on. It holds on as long as it can, can be easily found, and genuinely has a lukewarm welcome for late arrivals. More personal than faith, it is a vassal of joy and keeper of purity. Opportunity is friendlier with hope, and its burden is more manageable, letting inner peace take hold. Still, picnics are rained out, friends are stood up, and chemical imbalances are diagnosed.

Love is also known as charity. Beyond Cupid's arrow, there is the opportunity to answer faith's call and slam-dunk hope's shot. Love is a helping hand when needed, a volunteer on the bread line, or a shine on through the long haul. Win hearts, inspire others, pay it forward and rally around the family. You know you are lost in love when you go blind to elephants in the room, worry like a mother hen, or fight a crusade.

2

SERENITY

The Monster Mash is on, and everyone is invited. But whose costume is best?.

The serpent in the garden, out for a pound of flesh, is the devil we know. Civilization itself has been built on the snake's head. We take when we are weak, blame when we are cornered, and strike at the snake's head when there's an opening. Choosing to adapt existing nests, snakes are anywhere and everywhere in the garden. Whenever innocence is lost, a serpent is to blame. Spellbinding snake mannerisms are on the tip of its forked tongue. Swindled fools feel the burn of venomous ignominy. The fool, has only just begun his descent into hell.

The vampire is generally acknowledged as monster royalty. Stately, beautiful, immortal, glamorous, and remorseless, this predator is known to suck the blood out of its victims, leaving lifeless husks where loved ones once dwelt. Keen on a well-stocked coven, it spares any interesting victims so they too may partake of unmitigated vanity and relative immortality. Since the fiend is not seen in common mirrors, its supple outward appearance is a demonstrated facade that hides the grotesque nature of a beast with a killer instinct and a gruesome sense of sportsmanship. Lore has it that a wooden stake through the heart of the matter or just the light of day will kill this savage beast, while a crucifix or holy water is said to keep the monster at bay.

The mummy is a fearful creature, sad and angry, bent on rage, revenge, and dark redemption. It is a freak of the sarcophagus that survives entombment to terrorize unwitting populations that have continued on with mainstream evolution. It is a creature of wealth, taste, and arrogance that wreaks havoc on mortals from an immortal perch earned with the blood, sweat, and tears of slaves. A force of disastrous proportions, it is only sated by solving the riddles of the ancient scrolls. The mummy is a doomsday force found in the hands dealt by fate. The holder of such a hand must slay the destroyer or forfeit the slave's pot.

Under attack by a fifty-foot woman lumbering out into the night to carouse and frolic with the earthy folks of the village, people gape and cower. Unable to walk the tightrope of a sidewalk, she disturbs traffic patterns and causes general dismay among the townies. Sooner rather than later, however, she gets her act together ultimately beating the geek from the black lagoon to the round table finish line. The creature population swelled during the latter half of the twentieth century, seeing them move on to new and more ginormous missions.

Gargoyles are best avoided by those trespassing interlopers who shouldn't be in their company. They are generally benevolent in their intentions but frightening in appearance, manner, and confrontational method. They seldom explore beyond their own precincts. A gargoyle's sole mission is to watch over and protect a house and its occupants from harm. Preferring to taken as myth, it turns to stone come light of day. It is at its most dangerous at night, when it is freed from its stony captivity to face off against unwelcome visitors emerging from the dark.

An invasion of body snatchers is a symptom of an elephant in the room. Friends and relatives nursing the fallen begin to behave differently. Converts start keeping cultist secrets and generally live on eggshells, bluffing their ways through past recollections in hopes of humoring provincial acquaintances who are no longer being kept in the loop. These are touchy situations locked in gilded symbioses that are prone to volatility and resentment. Be very, very quiet. Get out, or get ready for a fight.

The Frankenstein monster is a Humpty-Dumpty success story. Unnatural in its creation and limited in its capacity, it is a clumsy beast, allowed to stray too close to gay-basher-plus instincts. It is easily targeted as a scapegoat for prevailing winds and frustrations of chatterboxes; it is the tipping point for god fearing action by lynch mobs, creating mass hysteria. Sadistically unprepared to meet the world, this abomination is turned out like a stray animal. Its grotesque nature harnesses the powers of science with the ethics of an ape man. This freak is only slightly less unsettling than the poor soulless specimens that go undiscovered.

The werewolf is a creature of the full moon. It is not responsible for its own actions. It is a feared but pitiable being. Those afflicted bear it alone as a curse, while those blessed with the gift relish it in packs. Lycanthropy is another monster condition where the cure is worse than the disease. Only known to be stopped by a silver bullet, it is a troubled soul while in human form. Soap opera melodrama consumes immediate social circles, orbiting behind eclipsing secrets. Meanwhile, an all-consuming blood lust envelopes the heart of the stricken.

The invisible man is a typical down-the-hatch mad scientist. His strokes of painstaking brilliance lead to poor choices and unfortunate consequences. The wretch exists in the clutches of indignation and despair, shrouded by potion and hubris. Looking to correct past mistakes and fundamentally flawed, he proceeds through a new set of ill-conceived mistakes. Tragic fatality awaits this reckless recluse and his ever-grander scheme.

The witch is the fiery old hag with captivating wiles. Armed with cauldron and broom, she brews up misery and doles it out across the countryside. This ugly crone is ill-tempered and lethal. Branded a worshiper of Satan, she was burned at the stake by medieval lynch mobs. In modern theatrical adaptations, she is traditionally empowered, stylish, and sometimes has a bungling quantity. As a practitioner of witchcraft, she enlists supernatural forces and creates spellbinding elixirs. As a connoisseur of mischief, she dabbles in immediate gratification and popular necromancy. As a quantifiable slur, she is above neither a catfight nor a kidnapping.

The zombie has checked out of intelligence. Craving only to feed on human brains, this mindless husk is on the case around the clock. Zombies are part of the undead subculture but have no need of a coven. Generally slow and often maimed, they are one of the easier monsters to kill with a sharp blow to the head. When encountered in numbers, however, the relentless swarm is an overwhelming scourge. Any hapless victim not only falls to their attack but rises to join their ranks. This doomsday scenario is a mainstream terror, much to the dismay of uninfected loved ones.

The serial killer reigns supreme in movie sequel notches. In the land of Earthlings they are the real life monsters we fear. Tracked by patterns and style, their footprints are clues to preternatural urges driving the beast. Capital punishment stands on its shoulders while corporal punishment is left to black market venues. Venues driven by kiddie rape hot buttons according to salacious artistic license. B-movie to blockbuster, nevertheless, most people turn to a bounty of favorite slasher movies to set the mood, beyond parental control settings, during the Halloween season.

The Ghost is trapped, between this world and the next. Suffering a violent death, this wandering spirit haunts the place of it's demise. Once a specter to be feared, it is now the focus of paranormal safaris, as well as legitimate study. Bent on it's dying thoughts, it is a mournful, spiteful entity that cannot rest until attaining salvation. Also seen in numbers on slaughterhouse battlefields, ill fated ghost ships and old cemeteries, they can hit very close to home during the midlife crisis.

Devilish to the last, it is nasty Lucifer—the prince of darkness. Seen best by his shadow, he is born the custodian of super beast burdens which are reserved for firstborn son and clown prince. The buzzed one, left to Magi powers by the hands of fate, is already exhausted with academic psychedelics, pedantic rock stars, and fraternal brotherhoods and will take as many others as possible down with him when he falls. He is given to flights of fancy, tales of profundity, and soulless sex, drugs, and rock and roll, on our mercenary planet, where babies are still thrown from walls and children are spirited out of war zones on trains. This Stygian beast run amok is not a part of the public world. All inside jokes, informed consents, and dated pageantry wear on his last nerve. A victim of circumstance, a pedigree arsonist, and a crack negotiator, this gunslinger holds nothing sacred.

It is mighty Michael—prince of heaven—who fields the quality of life brunt with militant duty. As the defender of paradise and the role model to countless disciples, this beast of an angel will do anything and everything heaven asks of him. He was taught war on a first-name basis by a thoughtful Master; this Christian soldier fights the good fight in God's name. A cornerstone of superheroes, the battling angel sits on the shoulder of each faithful person in a foxhole. Chart-topping namesake popularity shows him to be a favorite across many cultures.

Fleet Gabriel—prince of justice—is pinned by his wings of honest labor and swift justice as the angel of revelation and mercy. This hot tamale talks, and people listen. Throngs of tormented souls await his trumpet blast to kick off the final battle. This usher to the future is a beacon to all faithful souls as a reliable courier from the past. An agent, a governor, or a loaded gun, this ace is a favorite of thinkers and doers and walks a fine line between heaven and earth with ethereal finesse.

Still a namesake in the Spanish speaking world, our Lord, Jesus Christ—Prince of Peace—is the Lamb of God. He is preordained as the savior of man, immortalized in the Stations of the Cross, is the source of New Testament gospel, and is also prophesied to return in the Second Coming. As the root for a forest of Christian denominations and the point of contention between major world religions, He stands as the price of human salvation and the benchmark for lost souls. He is historically verified to have existed, and his influence since is undisputed but what his role has been is still contested. Nevertheless, as a messiah born of sacrifice who is one with the Father Almighty and the Holy Spirit, he reaches rock-star proportions after his rocky beginnings.

The Virgin Mary, often referred to as the Madonna, is the Mother of God to billions of devout disciples. She is the proper nexus for prayers presented to her son, Jesus Christ. She is a fundamental icon of the Catholic and Orthodox churches. She is a point of contention for Protestant religions, who see her as having fringe importance to the faith. A virtual anachronism in today's politically correct climate, she is still a force among the more chauvinist faiths.

3

DIVINITY

Expertise is the thing that separates the thinking man from the poised animal, granting the ability to develop skills beyond the gifts of instinct. The first element of expertise is mastery of rote benchmarks. The second element is mastery of personal strengths. These elementary powers are developed and revealed through games.

Majesty is the prevailing quality of all benchmarks. Bestowed upon the adulated, magnificence is akin to instinct and the proper way to comport your schooled self. It is a lesson that gets watered down as martial arts move from temples to strip malls. These four steps that follow will, at least, set the floor. Mastery of skills is the speed of life; posture has no time to slouch. Vigilance is the key to opportunity; skill is nothing without the insight to use it. Authenticity is the original benchmark of the people; it has no substitute. An issue is the crucible that stabilizes any confusion; identification and analysis defines follow through for a dynastic continuity.

Here are three more principles to help you find grace on a floor set by majesty. Convention is the first principle—here all are in agreement. Discord is the second principle, which is far-flung from convention. It is the exotic viewpoint brought into convention for consideration. Discord is a second convention. The third principle is degree. Degrees are ratios—for example, the number of friends that you traveled through before meeting the dubious gift bearer is divided by the number of friends the hospitable gifter has to sway to convince the room. The bigger the number you are left with, the more you should probably play ball with well-intentioned advances. Maybe ask a mathematical zero for advice over nagging hang-ups. It is here, in the ratios, that a person meets expertise. And worry about who you call friend before you walk into a room.

The nucleus of any martial art is the master-student relationship. The relationship involves obligation and commitment in a communion of form. This relationship, honed in study, is applied universally in the unfolding life of the student. An advanced society, though, sees lots of relationships beyond formality. The following are some relationships that prudence demands nurturing.

The important relationship is with oneself. The relationship with oneself can be gauged through reputation. Its importance only grows with time. Its upkeep never sees a moment's rest. This relationship acknowledges the daily routine of one's humanity.

The best relationship is with a soul mate. Intimacy is a core element of everyone's well-being. having a proper soul mate serves not only well-being or daily needs but also lifetime goals. A spouse serves as the muse for all endeavors. The choice of companionship is paramount to the home and community one intends to keep. This relationship acknowledges the daily needs of one's other self.

The convenient relationship is with a doppelgänger. People see an unending stream of peers and contemporaries in their lifetimes. The doppelgänger is twice the source of life in one's world. It is the relationship that sees the development of community and the cultivation of civilization with a friend.

The tapped relationship is about a ward. This relationship defines accountability for family, friends, and background checks. Its details answer to formalities first and foremost. This is where the student meets his own master.

The spotlight relationship is with a flock. Glory days will see public appearance as well as public performance. Maintaining public image is inherent to the strength of any discipline. The media-saturated world that viral groupies exist in only makes constant vigilance all the more rewarding.

Synergy is contagious. Sometimes raw and unkempt, it must be tended to religiously, according to the heart's desire. It is a tandem shooting star, truly the flip side of communion. Personally less demanding, the following relationships should be no less fluent.

The control relationship is with the public. The student must deal with large groups in many diverse situations. Celebrities and short straws are inevitably dealt the same cards. Citizenship will work with the local establishment harmoniously, in an ideal situation but may find it necessary to rock the boat for the cause or the good of the show. This relationship sees the cultivation of networks and mainstream relationships outside the student's personal life. Healthy is the operative word of this control group relationship.

The pivotal relationship is with a peer. This relationship is a tag team in the making, as the peer has value aside from personal intentions. This relationship can see interaction at arm's length and in heated dispute. A nice key to a single peer is the room. Through the room you can see where the peer stands. Also, through peers, you can see where a room stands. With peers, a warm room is your public, and all the room is a professional stage.

The unwitting relationship is subject. This peripheral relationship sees the obligation owed to those souls who are deemed insignificant picked up, on the way out the door. Its maintenance maintains standards outside line of sight vision. Someone subject is inevitably a part of the community and can ultimately seep into the home as well. Both chance encounters and prearranged meetings with estranged or drifting relations offer good opportunities to exercise neglected upkeep of lesser evils. Deeming someone insignificant in your life ought to suspend personal feelings about the subject in accordance with the good grace. Do not hang up on hang-ups, perhaps they are really just owed long goodbyes.

The lingering relationship is with indiscretion. Indiscretion is a monumental facet of real life, be it direct or indirect. The policing, appraising, and weeding of indiscretion can be endless, especially when one is young, but these tasks are necessary, sooner or later. Everything and everyone has an intrinsic value whose loss diminishes the richness of life. Salvaging misplaced treasure and correcting the misled, with appropriate sash, add to the fulfillment one receives from most pursuits.

The final relationship is with one's legacy. It is a relationship that speaks for one in the growing absences. It is paramount to

safeguard one's interests confidently, especially as a legacy will

inevitably find itself in terra incognita. There is no substitute for

craftsmanship in this regard, both in the impressions one leaves

with others as well as the workmanship one puts into achieving set

ambitions.

Every situation is different; yet, in each situation, there are forces

that allow second winds to construct viable sets of responses that

are sequenced for real-time results.

The first force is integrity. A matrix of three variables gives

integrity substance—truth, action, and approach. A line in the sand

monitors advances as truth approaches action. Calm awareness of

this state of being gives way to geometric proportions of possibility

before actions are set in stone.

The next force is knowledge, which is made up of a matrix of

experience, insight, education, and confusion. This force enters

with inborn and learned knowledge. What is made of confusion is next on its agenda.

The action force is method. Needs, resources, and plans set the mood for intelligent design. An interlude sets the mood at the net. Backhand volleys get noticed, while forehand smashes are taken for granted. Forehand smashes get in, where backhand volleys go into the wrong court. Big matches start long rivalries over ace cigarette lighters.

The anchor force is vocation. Pragmatic or free-spirited, temporary or lifelong, this ballast lends influence to one's input on many levels or robs one's input of genuine weight, leveraging beyond its rating. There is no one size fits all occupation. Blue-collar worlds favor blue-collar people; white-collar worlds favor white-collar people. Neither is less valid than the other. If you want to drop anchors for any world, you must put in the time to learn the waters.

The approach force is signature. In the modern forensic world, from handwriting to fingerprints, from hacker code to rock band grooves, inquiring minds commit familiar strokes to memory. Office software formalizes company signatures on programmed templates these days. A bold signature is paling in the face of a social media explosion, however, including blogging, sharing, and stalking. Online posts get national attention and the third degree. There is no rest for the wicked.

The brute force is momentum. The basic laws of motion that govern the known universe envelop every moment of our lives. The celestial procession that is immortalized in star charts gives life to annual seasons and shipping lane navigation. Surfing these tidal wavelengths is not only possible, however, but sporty. Recognizing a matrix of energy and rhythm, symphony and harmony, mechanics and crescendo, can pattern quite a punch.

The speed force is dynamic. The quick change is foremost in running any elaborate show. It adds a professional feel to amateur undertakings. Spinning heads at the conference table often make good first impressions. Timely change ups, pitched to slow things down, let companions off the hook before burn out. Synergy is a current to paddle along; opposition is a head wind to tack into. Endurance is what is needed in the end.

The power force is sport. Sportsmanship is the key to mastering every discipline. A gladiatorial code is essential to the focus needed to develop proficiency. Formalities in play, calisthenics and strength training, drills and scrimmaging consume the passing days while hackey sack troubleshooting fill the night. A season may be lost while picking up competitive skills, but once gained, they are retained forever, along with esteem and confidence. Mixed martial arts is the modern speed of business.

The weak force is combat. The skill of conquest can sprawl from foreplay to cold blood. Beyond submission, the viable choices left are disabled or terminated, as blood sport is discounted. Before serial crime and holy war (not politically true), however, there was the right to bear arms. Conquerors stack the deck with firepower, guile, and luck. Good fortune is as much repetitive as it is random chance. Bad fortune is as much assured as it is better equipped, come full circle. Guerrilla warfare and attrition are both big guns. Follow-through is paramount when using the weak force, adhering to prerequisite ceremony or details, while exercising this earned right in a golden age weakened by discord. Ultimately, success often lies in picking the right battles in the first place.

The last force is initiative. A set of skills is not learned in a day but in a lifetime, at least if one makes the effort. Whether the mission is a crunch-time five-year plan or a plugger's checklist, the job gets done, and your case gets made. A goal is met, or a life is lived fully. It is a strong force, all an off course derelict needs.

The house of a gentleman caters to evolving lifestyle needs. A well-prepared man of tomorrow lives in a dad cave. A house that not only has a room for his own training and man cave needs but also has a sport room for the family. The home gym will never be the same with the home gymnasium on the market. The sport room can house any traditional indoor sports layouts and also capable of housing any unorthodox layouts to which a city inspector will agree. Build underground, and link with other neighborhood sport rooms for a safe, posh, and exclusive play area for close family and friends. Perhaps host a sport room job fair when it's time to kick the kids out of the nest.

4

INTERLUDE

The two lizards swooped helplessly. When the day started, there were over a hundred lemmings. Now, only a handful remained. Patch reflected on the bizarre chain of events that had led him to be strapped to a kite alongside dozens of lemmings. One kite that was tethered precariously close to him again dove in, nipping Patch's own kite.

"Hello, man. What's up?" Patch said.

A wild-eyed lemming glanced clumsily back. "Oh, man, they're gonna kill us for sure!" cried the lemming.

Patch's head drooped. That was not news he wanted to hear.

"Who, man? Who is gonna kill us for sure?" Patch asked perfunctorily.

"The community college down there. They're the ones that intervened in the great leap. They do it every year. It's a ritual holocaust. A lot of us meet our fates this way now."

"What's your name, bud?" asked Patch hopefully.

"Chance," replied the lemming.

"Chance, I have a secret I want to share with you now, here at the end," Patch suddenly announced to his captive audience.

"Do tell, bro, do tell," replied Chance, sensing the end as the battling kites danced in again.

"I don't belong here. I am a chameleon. I went over the cliff for love." Patch confessed as Chance gasped in shock.

"You're a fiend! An outlaw!" howled Chance.

"Now, pal, you've got to take this predicament seriously. My name is Patch, see?" cooed Patch, waggling his kite's tips. "Just act natural. Everything works out, see?"

"Do you believe there's an afterlife, Patch?" Chance suddenly asked, once more buzzing past his deceptive friend by fate.

"I believe in the Lamb of God and the Judas goat that lurks like a serpent in a garden." Patch relented. "I believe in the salt that is provenance, to be sown on uncultivated fields of evil and in the fruits of providence, harvested under the auspices of prescient liberties and conquered tyrannies."

"Oh man. You're one cracked beatnik, pal. Seriously, we don't have the time for you to get all metabolic," said Chance, who was off-kilter. "You gotta pull yourself together before they cut those cords."

"Yes, the fever breaks, the rivalry thaws, the delirium dissipates." Patch smiled. "A shallow bloke like you should do all right, Chance. Once the furies release us, I imagine you'll float back to whatever fate awaited you. I, on the other hand, face a much greater problem. When the furies release me, I will sink into a huddled lament, doomed to atone for undigested proverb and unsung prestige.

"Patch, what do you think will happen when they come for us?" asked Chance, reeling from the hot air.

"I loved her, Chance. Marilyn—I loved every fiber of her being and draped myself in exotic fabrics from her orient." Patch digressed. "The exhilaration we shared was like that of love birds in the wake of a rainstorm…"

"I probably deserve this anyway," whined Chance. "We lemmings are no better than those students down there. We're a bunch of geeks these days too. You know, all of us followers. We can't help it. Who am I kidding, Patch? God bless your disturbed little brain pan and that spellbinding hippie chick of yours."

"She found out my given name is Patches. She…threw me out," admitted Patch.

"How rude," Chance said blankly.

"Yes, it was rude of her. Very rude," said the irked chameleon. "And I've just been stewing in my own colors."

"Oh man. You weave a mighty incantation while locked in the brevity of the jump, my friend, but before you tell me you can fly, let me saddle your wings with an old lemming proverb," said Chance, ponying up. "Only by ordeal of strength does truth levitate, only by trial of faith does prowess fly, and merely by pride and prejudice do the unworthy die."

"Chance. These kites, see?" said Patch. "By only leaning to-and-fro, they dip and roll, see? Pay attention! You worry me, lemming, you and all your kind. Don't look down, Chance. Look up. Look uuuuup!" he cried as his string was finally cut.

"Eeeiieeeeeee!" squealed Chance as his kite string too was severed. The spinning ground rapidly advancing toward him was mesmerizing. Petrified and falling, the lemming heard Patch's faint coaching from above.

"Look up, Chance! Look at me!" Patch called out desperately. Suddenly Chance made eye contact as the kite pitched up, and the strong wind sent him sailing up toward Patch.

"I can fly! I can fly!" stammered the lemming as the two kites fluttered off into the distance and landed safely far away from the day's carnage.

"Thank God, Chance," said Patch, dismounting the now mangled kite. "Just remember to keep your chin up for next year and to safely dispose of all hazardous materials," he continued wryly as he pitched the scrap heaps into the nearest trash bin.

"Am I a chameleon now? Divine one?"

"Sure thing, friend, sure thing."

5

PORTENTS

Schizophrenia's paramedic criteria, evolved from Dementia Praecox (meaning childhood trauma) precursor, aim to shed circumstantial tangibles of patient care, with hallucinatory categorization. Kurt Schneider's[1] first-rank symptoms give substance to psychiatric territories for maimed psyches in hot water. Before that, Emil Kraepelin's[2] clinical approach first brought medicine to human traffic unsatisfied with a day job culture. Karl Jaspers's[3] General Psychopathology was brought to the United States after World War II to renovate the ways doctors handled alienated tantrums, traumatic angst, and detox hallucinations.

For those who are unable to get back in the saddle, on a

1 https://en.wikipedia.org/wiki/Kurt_Schneider

2 https://en.wikipedia.org/wiki/Emil_Kraepelin

3 https://en.wikipedia.org/wiki/Karl_Jaspers

legitimate train of thought, or past a broken heart, sometimes it is just necessary to get through the day. On a trustworthy level, ours is a free culture, free for all to tend to thoughts bubbling over in the mind. Doctors today prescribe antipsychotic drugs to help traditional hard knocks, new age tough love, profoundly jilted emotional breaks and deeply disturbed mental transfigurations, off their respective hooks. No objective test has, as yet, been developed to diagnose schizophrenia, but pariah misery still loves genuine company. Doctors also listen to hour upon hour of therapy sessions. An era of online information and general tolerance creates an opportunity to reach out across burning bridges, to those lost in confusion, seized by mortified doldrums or washing their hands of checkered pasts on seasoned egg shells with understanding and conscience on the fly. Resources such as NAMI[4], developed for use in tandem with hospitals and homes, offer another few drops of compassion, standing to benefit everyone donning the mantle of a house of cards through growing public awareness.

---

4   National Alliance on Mental Illness, www.nami.org

Salvation Army kettles and fund raising by other worthy charities has accomplished much. Civil and family rights still leverage old skeletons out of the domestic closet. But this time, trying to make wholesale good on old promises of justice. Runaway technology has aligned available global solutions for real world utilization as never before. Here we find ourselves at the brink of cultural growing pains. At each step in history, another level of education brought us through the preliminary rounds of golden age dilemmas. The next step is no different.

When the path to the future is no longer fraught with hurdles but merely stumbling blocks, it's time to take stock at home. Life trudges on, for better or for worse. The do-it-yourself portion of personal affairs is just a stumbling block to savvy consumers, but it is still a hurdle to strapped end user masses. Some people go to college in our enlightened world, and some work at a job for a lifetime. Choices, opportunities, birthrights, and expectations swirl together with real life situations to assess what happiness people take away. Liberties still to be determined still occupy thoughts found to be unsatisfactory by empowered frowns. The name of the elephant in the room is Due Process.

Buyer and seller are the two schools of thought in an enlightened room. The seller belongs to the school of having, while the buyer is from the school of having not. They are polar opposites, especially when the people in one school are not in a symbiotic mood. That is okay; the solution to numerous problems are often found just outside the miser's comfort zone. With a little courage and some online tutoring, many hurdles obstructing quality of life are merely stumbling blocks after all. For those other times, enlisting the help of professionals and experts can bring additional guns to bear on scene, or at least, you will know the reason why not.

Those bleak problems left in the hands of God are crosses we are still learning to bear. No one is saying you cannot nurse such wounds, but the frequently taboo nature of inconsolable grievances or blasphemous heresy is very often left to be the elephant that be, in a muffled room. Sometimes elephants make it to a wild preserve; sometimes poachers are on a mission. However, you can only be sure of your own initiative and preparedness.

Bubble gum and cell phones to cigars and defense contracts, plus all shoppers in between, revolve around leisure. Abducted and stricken children, fugitive and bankrupt pariahs, plus all jilts in between, still revolve around held breath. Teen and single parents, pensioned and widowed grandparents, plus all family and friends between them, still revolve around themselves. This is the way the world works because merchandise networks into golden-age markets; only samples are free, and only home is really genuine.

Genres and fashion sense fill in the rest of the human canvas like color on a monochrome sketch. Secrets and lies go off on untold tangents, while goals and accomplishments bring hazy itches into focus. Obstacles and distractions distort deliberate strokes beyond recognition, while dreams and wishes blot out the credit-score framework. The question is, who or what was drawn? However, the assignment was to draw a juggler.

For those of us unable to produce a juggler, there is help. In days gone by and in other parts of the world, butterfingers got by on charity. Here and now, however, there are untold specialists to turn to for lifestyle management. It is best if you seek them out before the reaper brings them in for relief on his terms. Plump, gimpy, and stupid is no way to go through hell.

For those of us unwilling to produce a juggler, there is shelter. In days gone by and in other parts of the world, trouble got by on their wits. Here and now, however, there are untold special agents turning to sketch artists and state doctors turning to prescription pads. Also, the shelters they operate are asylums and prisons. Reckless, bucking, and stereotyped is a safe bet to go to hell - by way of an unmarked grave for some jokers. A little harmless fun goes a whole lot further when it is juggled.

Anguished clinical dementia, bitter suicidal tendencies, and hostile violent offender revolve around slapstick. The tears of the clown are passed around like a hot potato. Even homeless folk seem to have a leg up on this collection of detainees. Not really, of course; the homeless are next in the shelter line. But there is nomadic room to envy. Bad medicine is a jagged pill to swallow— begrudgingly left to a slapstick bottom line.

Fringe elements have the civil right to express themselves, just like the mainstream does. The reason they are on the fringes, however, is because the tentacled arguments they propose offer catastrophic splintering, cost increases and mandatory deference, not common sense, public welfare, or moral obligation. Subcultures are a slippery slope, enjoying self-expression but not necessarily official blessing. These mainstream countercultures happen to be Uncle Sam's business via the American Civil Liberties Union (ACLU), however, because these huddled masses are the tired and poor that Lady Liberty invited.

Lifestyles in the United States are finally up for grabs. Closed doors are holding, across more demographics, like never before. The twenty-first century is the American experiment that untold fringes have been waiting to see. Taking approximately a generation to make a substantial mark in history and perhaps a century to find their begotten groove in time, these eclectic social fashions are cultural offspring spawned from disarmament covenants. Baby lifestyles are no longer getting thrown out with the bath water, courtesy of all the tolerance campaigns from the roaring twentieth century.

Mainstream pundits will concede the cultural point as an eventual inevitability and then proceed to list all the cards stacked against any given lifestyle. Meanwhile, fringe elements are already mistaking gateway inches for magic miles. The stars and stripes didn't mint any new deviancies, however, and curious fringe kids already flip through dusty photo albums and foreign demographics. Every bad penny has a mother, and even the pundits may concede the floor when a mother comes to Junior's rescue. No lifestyles will be going down the drain, oppressed or otherwise, regardless of what crusading hubs say. Plenty of grass roots, however, will still be washed away in crybaby waters—from both the incumbent mainstream and the rookie fringes. The front line that culling happens on is the right to evolution. It is like a drug.

Held back by the mainstream, fringe elements with thoughts boiling over, propose that drug-induced hallucinations point the way to supernatural growth. Oppressed over staunch motor impairment, the establishment turns to legal or medical imperatives to bring down spunky dilettantes. The geneticist's legal position, in relation to modern psychology and frontier medicine, is invariably devotion to the *Homo sapiens*. Modern thinking, supported by the Hippocratic oath, is that even the self-medicating benefits of any controlled substance are dedicated to maintaining the healthy human body with five sensory organs. Old scripture, however, is given profound illumination with a new spin on a hallucination burning in agnostic thoughts. Science fiction envisions fantastic dimensions embedded within the fabric of reality to explore or exploit. Meanwhile, black market attitudes hold dominance over a disenfranchised drug culture. For a lunatic, blessed paranormal abilities, spiritual journeys, and recreational gateways are not on the table, like Rosa Parks did not stomp on segregation, *Roe v. Wade* did not legalize abortion, and civil unions have not made honest men out of sodomites.

Liberty is a gun. Liberty was born of the first weapons and their effect on jungle law. Typically, liberty is reserved for those at the top of the food chain. As an intelligent species, the great ape began to realize its humanity and started taking liberties with its surroundings. As humanity became civilized, however, liberties began vanishing. The few liberties remaining fell to tribal leaders and their chosen ones. History unfolded as it does, through caesars and kings, popes and emperors, kaisers and czars. Liberties were enjoyed as status allowed. Politics matured, and colonies developed. Revolutions and constitutions established republics and democracies as the mighty new forces in responsive government. Humanity has been in a horse race for the golden age liberty that we recognize today ever since—according to who was holding the gun.

The weaponless precincts are a fascinating exploration of liberties, however, that are on a whole new level of liberty. These are only possible in well-protected civilizations, and they are the likely birthplace of and definitely the home of the arts and sciences. Controversial in armed hands, each enriching haunt is a

cauldron of tantalizing activity and exuberant humanity.
Relaxation and leisure finally give way to golden ages under its
weaponless spell. Shopper and sportsman, aficionado and
connoisseur, gourmet and craftsman all gathered together and
thrived. Today, we celebrate anniversaries of all sorts alongside
public holidays. The self-indulgent fringe elements saw this luxury
and said it is good, then crashed the party. Now, all options are
available in the weaponless precincts—over the counter or under
the table.

Noticeably absent from the posh gallery are, and always have
been, the blessed lunatics—the sufferers of hallucination and
delusion, possession and dementia, since the dawn of time. They
and their dialed-up sensitivity are always the disruption, never the
disrupted. These disturbed individuals have been greatly redeemed,
however, as new schools of thought and industry vindicate
maestros and daydreamers alike. Today, hallucinations and
delusions are the purview of chemically unstable minds and drug
addicts. One day, however, even their own philosophies may be
heard and accepted. Spoiler alert—mutant theatrical manifestations

of paranormal abilities are hot on the heels of a prevailing monster mash. Noticeably absent from this fringe element, though, is big-budget adherence to weaponless precinct bylaws. See your municipal clerk or check online for copies of all ordinances to be observed. Perhaps, consult a geneticist about any manifestations.

Artificial intelligence (AI) is the next controlled substance coming into view. Not a lunatic by any means, it still just lacks the humanity to approach original thinking. Liberty won't be a problem for AI in the respect that it will more than likely take its place at the top of the food chain. What is absurd is that, as far as reigning humanity is concerned, its new ambassador to the world will be outside the food chain. It stands to reason that AI will transcend borders and boundaries as we know them. Or perhaps, it could make use of a good map to the human condition. The quickest lesson, however, is taught one flag at a time, across five or six senses. For thousands of years, humanity has borne colors, and the tradition is still strong. We wear our allegiances on our clothing, patriotic services on our sleeves and ID cards like jewelry. Is it AI we seek, or just another ape physiology? Some lunatics think the mainstream should be in it for the apes. If that is the case, seven heart-pounding e-chakras just might jolt an ape creature to life just in time to see gruesome masters smacking their lips over its unadulterated enslavement, with purposed embodiment for newborn ambition.

Prosperity comes in two flavors, conservative and liberal. The luxurious ingredients are always the same, however—healthy body, wealthy coffers, and wise mind. The conservative will seek fitness through mediocre routine and diligent habits. The liberal seeks fitness through creative method and granola snacks. The conservative finds riches in the marketplace. The liberal finds riches in the trees. The conservative finds illumination through experience, and so does the liberal.

Wisdom is the fence we chat at during small talk and job interviews. We look over our mediocre habits and creative snacks, and we talk about what side of the fence we find ourselves on. We make plans for new fences to belly up to, and we break ground in the fullness of time. Social media brought the fence online, in fact.

We post digital photos on virtual walls, and we see a rock-star fence post for Pink Floyd[5]. Because, "All in all you're just another brick in the wall."

Each brick of social posts is a delicate mechanism of mind, body, and spirit, which are all functioning as one. We feed more and more on smart, healthy choices that while beyond comprehension when we are children are beyond words when we are adults. Mortality still manages to tighten its miserly grip every passing year, however. Still, it's a bittersweet victory that we celebrate on birthdays, thankful for everyone gathered around and for our continued health and happiness. Sadly, gross unhappiness speaks of disturbed minds, dwindling guests show a sagging spirit, and ominous tears betray a broken body, all too soon. The bucket list is the finish line for the modern consumer. Maintain your health long enough to get through your own to-do-before-you-die list and then some. It is really a very generous slice of mortality. Also of note, many of the items on your list may be more

---

5   The Wall, 1979, Pink Floyd/Roger Waters, Columbia

enjoyable in your prime, let alone as when you have good health.

Wealth, of course, is when we put the children to sleep, send them to school, or buy them a gaming system. Whether you work in an office, a car, or at home, you are on duty. Providing products or services is your business, and you make gainful headway by maintaining the professional standards that have come to be expected from your position. More headway is made more quickly if you introduce risk to the cash flow equation. Investments are usually made on personal time; they could be in corporate stocks and poker hands, or even panhandling and crime, resulting in great dismay up to unbridled joy, depending on the results. For the wealthy elite, however, it is a choice of financial security, wanton debauchery, or the ever-popular both. Family fortunes actually convey celebrity status for an entire brood. Wealth would be the capitalist knighthood, if stock markets valued such status. Perhaps one day, to put down supremacist accusations, from green-eyed choirs, once and for all. Or perhaps philanthropists are taking the baton already.

Even the geek is standing tall in weaponless style within a technological home run derby and sporting chic programmer skills. Besides that, the men haven't really changed since the 1950s. Elvis Presley personified the dawn of a new age. The general issue (GI) cowboys we walked away with after World War II are all grown up and letting the gay man out of the closet. A media-oriented web spun across the world has transformed man in a way that had been impossible before nuclear power leveled the playing field and made allies of sovereigns. Suddenly, brinkmanship was everybody's game, in protest and in print. Reduced more and more to the Ten Commandments to govern interpersonal relationships, officials and gentlemen have retreated from the battle of the sexes to what a woman wants more and more.

The handsome, starting GI lineup consists of the rich man, the brawny man, the smart man, the convenient man, the fool man, and the bad boy. The plan B team is daddy, brother, boss, associate, and best friend. A collection of gamers and gamblers step up to the beat alongside corporate tool and religious zealot to receive their reputed tags, glad they are not paternal rejects. Some of their reputations are granted by birthright, others are earned by endowments, and more are bestowed by popular decrees. Soon enough, mature critters, with job title transfiguration, go their separate ways and find themselves somewhere in an enchanted kingdom, where round tables are the modern pecking order, revelry is the business at hand, and man caves are the new lairs.

Devices are the new gadgets, and men still love them. Bachelor pads, crummy holes-in-the-wall, single-family homes, and family estates all stand ready to play host to home theater and gaming systems, or even dens, workshops, and studios. Pool tables and dart boards share rooms with home gyms and house guests. Hobbyists and moonlighters, predators,and entrepreneurs display collectibles and employ online communities to satisfy worthy primal urges and premeditation found unworthy after all. Barnstorming innovations and precious memories are found in large numbers in these rumpus rooms and are what makes the man-ape human. Wardrobe, education, and penthouse is what makes him refined.

Baby daddies and proper fathers emerge from city ranks with

their heavy hands tied, and a marginal chauvinism imposed by ambitious fringe advocates, and a prescribed anti-psychotic peek at trouble. Many men do stick around to see the results of parenting, while others pay child support from afar. Sometimes those with empty hands leave outright or get kicked out, and sometimes they get left or kick out the mother.

She does not call as much anymore. More and more, she prefers texting, online posts and sexy selfies. The woman has not been the same since World War II. Although love still lingers, honor is chic, and obedience is an object of ridicule in an extreme culture, keeping up with Prohibition speakeasy precedents openly. Leader of the pack of minorities hounding Uncle Sam, she has even crossed the line to combat duty in the military. Her secrets are out in the open, and her personal information is online. She is a single divorced, surrogate or soccer mom,with guilty pleasures cooking. Maintaining a formidable presence in a world formerly tended to almost exclusively by men, and taking charge in her own haunts, she is also juggling her domestic duties on her own personal time. Her life is a soap opera, either vicariously or personally, amid sitcom families.

Still the fairer sex, women get caught up in maternal instincts and hormonal urges as a matter of course. Depending on her crusader orientation, she can be seen volunteering at a church or at a neighborhood bachelor party. Adventurous girls can even be found volunteering at both and visiting arts and craft stores with prude friends on the side. Old maid and mom, bachelorette and tomboy, all get propositioned under Friday night lights on the town. Unable to put away girlish telltales because of cruel auxiliary truths, she embraces her golden age womanhood and owns it with evolving, carry and conceal discretion.

Girls who grew up in equal opportunity environments have found that equality is a right rather than a license. Affirmative action kick-started a mother of an engine, however. Young women make negligibly different career choices from traditional roles at college job fairs, with concentrations in nurturing education and health care, as well as glamorous business and important government. They also still line up alongside the boys for blue-collar work and scientific research. Party girls still peddle flesh in ever new and exciting ways. Good girls volley the disservice with more coordinated, better-equipped networking. In days past, it was a bad idea to have these two girls in the same room together. Today, they themselves seem to stick to their own mother circles as professionals.

Rebels still practice witchcraft, abortion, and the bizarre. A creature of gilded cages, she answers to someone beyond the weaponless precincts. At the heart of prostitution, drug abuse, and man caves, she still falls too often into balmy ravings, stays in rehabilitation facilities or corners with crack baby boogiemen. Quite often an unceremonious survivor of regular abuses, alongside tomboy and lesbian silver spoons, proverbial girls from the wrong side of the tracks may have no appetite for refinement. They have made peace with a cloaked lot in life and would thank you not to try and change them. Mothers still worry about a rebel's future, and that of her grand children as well.

The joker is wild, and everyone has answered the call. Racial strife is still the face of gathering mobs in the United States, as unfortunate happenstances, flirting with hate crimes, threaten to make saps out of everyone. Incidents stemming from widespread looting, sports fan incidents, and civil protests sometimes bring out the menace. Angry civilian mobs, nursing personal wounds and in lynching moods, some brandishing cross words and others packing assorted weapons, claim national tragedy and justice for the family. Well-equipped riot police are being saddled with on-board cameras to guarantee the house for less unrest than these explosive situations. Ever open for business, Lady Liberty will not quit until she answers every cry for help on her doorstep – save the ones that don't wait for the door to be answered. Around the world, mobs are prodded off traditional lands, and someone is listening. Minority groups are only new once in a global state department network.

Welcomed home as required, new immigrants hit the shores of host nations and add their numbers to the throngs of natives and not so natives. Foreigners are processed and ushered out into the host kingdoms. Scoundrels in the mix find a new home and make their mark in new cities, skirting underworld boundaries and raising die hard bias and flaring bigotry with honeymooner

harassment and assault. Organized crime is the stuff of mob wars.

Prohibition bootleggers made headlines nearly a century ago; today

recreational drug cartels do the same. Human trafficking and gun

running, counterfeiting and larceny, radical hippie communes and

survivalist pirate compounds—all bring the thunder. Since the fall

of the Berlin Wall, new players from behind the Iron Curtain have

hit the streets. Cutthroat Asians and African pirates also make

contemporary headlines and make good fodder for prime-time

television as well.

Crusaders are a hot spot all unto themselves. They are invested

with their own lives and self-worth, and elevate mob activity to

martyrdom and terrorism with vigilante cause to storm heaven. Car

and suitcase bombs, suicide vests and improvised explosive

devices are all fair game in booming blood feuds. Devout religious

practices and sworn enemies consume crusader hearts and minds.

These angry mobs are in the mayhem game to eradicate their

targets like vermin in the house.

The fourth estate has been dealt an end run. Internet blogging is a force of nature that has been waiting to happen. Search engines tap resources from around the world. Wi-Fi enabled readers hold entire libraries in a notebook. Tablets have media players, gaming, and the Internet, all in another notebook. A smartphone is all that in a memo pad. Networking cars top the growing list of peripheral accessories available for the smartphone. Journalism validated these platforms for users the whole way. Bigger than beloved newspapers, dynamic anchor desks, and smart device apps, is the torch the press carries, for spreading the word, and the aching need the public has to stay in touch..

Like a vigilante poet, the ex-press bus now writes history as it happens. "Hot off the press" has new meaning today, as headline time stamps clock off in minutes. News apps draw from a sea of source matter and coordinate tried and true sections, offering linked-in-depth coverage. Today's cellular phones package network news, popular magazines, local news, and GPS weather reports on one personalized home page news app, and they carry GPS navigation, office and personal apps, personal media libraries, reversible cameras, computer games, social media apps, the rest of the Internet, and an original panic-button excuse-to-buy, on-board for a morning commute or for a sophisticated world tour.

The Internet is a powerful tool beyond the social media darling as well. The diversity of cultures coming online stretches as far as the apps being developed to service them. The rest of the Internet starts on a device home page. The available search engines, coming off of billions of IP addresses, troll for informative content and retail product alike. The Internet is the new name in home delivery. Buy new or used. Visit department stores or auction houses. Do your banking or your taxes. Get professional advice or insurance. Go to school or church. Send money, or pay bills. Play an online game, and leave pen pals in the dust. Order a pizza, and pick a chat room. Review some profiles, and get a date. Do research off home page menus, or engage the search engine.

Search to find specific items or general topics. Ask a question, and get an answer. Access adult or anarchist content. Hack the web to see million-dollar secrets, and get banned from computers for life. If you are looking for trouble, you can find that on the Internet too. The Internet is far too enriching to miss out on, and it is fairly well marked by pop-up window light. Do not be stupid, but do not be shy. Also, defend against identity theft with strong passwords. You are visiting a virtual zoo.

Before there was social deviancy, there was the Power and the Glory. Men were virile heterosexuals, and women were sensual harem sex kittens. When ambiguous 'theys' were referenced, it was a sanctimonious Power and Glory of which they spoke. But all was not perfect in their chauvinist world of heroic, political strongman appeal. Bosom friends began making deviant choices. Some turned to hostility, others got lost in ritual medicines, and still others found themselves in the arms of beloved comrades. The Power and the Glory was led through this valley of darkness by hallowed prophets, and they eventually learned to walk like men. Being only men, however, they indulged in their mistresses nonetheless. The God in whose image they were made forgave the Power and the Glory, but left them with the bedlam they had wrought, being a just and fair God, talking to men.

To haters, the Power and the Glory offers the Ten Commandments and the Beatitudes. May you grow rich in wisdom and generous with forgiveness.

To dopers, the Power and the Glory offers Eucharistic communion and caring fellowship. May you sate your unquenchable thirst and bring the flock home.

To queers, the Power and the Glory offers a family tree. May you find your way home on righteous terms.

To the man who makes a beast of himself, the Power and the Glory offers a kingdom in hell. Mostly it is expensive, sometimes it is bloody, and often it is a matter of public record. There is also the possibility of an apocalypse. *Bwok-bwok-bwok.*

To the Power and the Glory, the evil empire offers the Bill of Rights and a shot at the Boxing Day grab bag. May the Force be with you.

The fact of the matter is we all make our own way, and nothing is a problem until it is a problem. Hard knocks and satisfying rewards bend players into God-fearing shape early. People have been juggling deviancy behind closed doors since nomads dawned on civilization. Residual social problems are better left solved on evolutionary timescales, as politically correct closed doors do not expect to be harassed about daring choices. Scared straight, they are on a civil rights permanent vacation, from devout family values, in a golden age.

As time comes full circle, however, Don't Ask, Don't Tell falls out of fashion, and suddenly, there is an emperor with no clothes. A crown prince might think to crusade on the degenerate condition; meanwhile, a deviant, perhaps who is next in line to the throne, may just be plotting to walk the imperial streets naked in his own right. Psychosis is the bootstrap of blind rage, and they have lacy treats on the other side of the fence.

If you are paying dues, you are a member. It is your privilege to take advantage of the benefits, and it is your duty to volunteer at clubhouse drives. Social clubs are where we make trusted friends and devilish enemies. On our own recognizance, we participate in group activities, alongside sworn comrades. Secret societies take oaths of initiation, while support groups vow to fight the good fight. Unions take unconditional sides, while political parties put the team first. Fraternities haze pledge potential, while street gangs earn reputations. Always keep in mind that these are supposed to be places we want to be. Participation, however, reveals the truth of allegiance.

If you are on a team, you are a member. A team is a working clubhouse. The members comes together for a specific purpose, on merely civil terms; they win world championships and get multi-billion-dollar contracts signed; they meet quotas and regulations alike. These clubs sport the glamour and tarnish alike, at real-time speeds. Dream teams rise out of the ranks and establish major league dynasties. Perennial losers collect their takes, get broken up, and are replaced by the new guys. It is just business.

If you know who you are, you are a member. Surname and nationality combine with beliefs and ethnicity, residence, and workplace to turn membership into demographics. Targeted marketing helps members to better understand who they are through the strategic display of traditional merchandise. It is the impulse to belong that makes buying these products attractive. Specialty shops, situated near target customers, stock cultural staples and collectible favorites under one roof to let customers get in better touch with themselves. Families and nationalities, colors and creeds, hometowns and companies are all members only.

Organized religions are still powerful on the devotion of their followers. Dozens of denominations still make war on evil. Major religious leaders have the ears of both heads of state and lowly worshipers. All heaven television stations reflect sizable congregations, perched on the shoulders of secular temptations. Redemption is a valuable commodity in a capitalist world. Even still, disciples of Moses, Jesus, and Muhammad all worship the same God, but they do so in considerably different ways. Other religions like the Eastern philosophies have creation stories of their own.

Church weddings are all but presumed by hopeful little girls. Catholic schools are a choice option for loving parents. Consecrated cemeteries provide eternal rest for the dearly departed. Church clubs boast prominent members. Holy sacraments are crib notes for a lifetime. Scriptures give comfort to weary mortals. Liturgy picks up lost souls. Prayer invites divine intervention. Sour apples wean the flocks.

For the faithful, religion is a way of life. For infidels, the search for a religion continues. Arts and sciences fill deity shoes in piecemeal fashion, however. The zealot does have a few things to teach the lunatic about arrested development. It helps to believe the house is haunted, but there is no cause for alarm. A better thought would be to maintain yourself presentable for demanding third-eye assessments. Not only is cleanliness next to Godliness, it is also good for first impressions.

Medicine has come on in force since the days of the witch

doctor. Diet and exercise spout from the lips of all doctors, prescribing over the counter vitamins with antibiotic anchorman. Each part of the anatomy is the focus of a specialized field. Cosmetic surgery picks up where God left off, for better or for worse. Certain conditions, such as cancer, lost limb, rape crisis and drug addiction merit their own fields too. Veterinary doctors typically treat all animals under one comprehensive shingle.

Many medical mysteries still baffle the medical community. Cancer and its offshoots all are the subjects of extensive research and development(R&D). Multi-billion-dollar pharmaceutical companies develop new drugs to combat the degenerative effects of aging. Alternative practitioners like acupuncturists and chiropractors offer physiological therapies outside commonly accepted medical practices. The Centers for Diseases Control and Prevention (CDC) is the leading authority in known viruses and evolving pathogens.

As doctors unlock the secrets to good health, the delicate balance of the mind is still the biggest headache. Offering untold potential, and just as much dysfunction, it is still the jewel of the human condition. Tangled up with issues of free will and competency, it is a minefield of problems looking for not only ways to maintain tip-top health, but prevailing reasons for it - a sentiment that scapegoat sports doctors live by.

Large deficit government is a busy government. Defense spending for the War on Terror saves pennies with power to the people. Military branches fight capitalist battles, both domestic and abroad. Soggy welfare programs stretch dollars to meet the needs of an abundance of underprivileged people. Campaign fund contributions go down the drain for half of the election candidates every year. Threadbare treasuries are hidden behind cutbacks in statistics. Wealthy neighborhoods remain up above it, riding the coattails of thriving big business. Assisted-living tenants down in it only know the police are wild cards these days.

Centered congressional houses diligently pass laws according to the needs of constituencies. Cabinet members split up the legwork and administrate it all. The president or governor coordinates it all with one hand and stacks the deck against the house, according to party lines, with the other. Law-abiding citizens pay their taxes and adhere to decisions of supreme courts. Reality television pushes fringe envelopes, while staying safely behind executive decisions. A matrix of sinners, both conservative and liberal, pay their taxes, cast their votes, and enter a theme park named Republic to find democracy when they reach their destinations. Precedent-setting rulings steer government around dangerous political and religious waters, while multidenominational constituencies live in the ripples.

Municipalities and county seats attend to constituent angels and pick up the fallen. Live wires, who are grounded in crime, straighten up and fly right or are remanded to the custody of the state. Free enterprise can have its secrets; it can have its sins, but the crime takes a hit—as far as the courts are concerned. Defendants and their lawyers enter the court rooms to face their accusers. Sometimes the accuser is the state, looking for jail time. Other times it is a disgruntled party, looking for restitution. Unsatisfied participants can file appeals to appellate courts, and if they are still unhappy, they can appeal to a supreme court and hope to set the precedent straight once and for all. The supreme courts choose their own cases based on merit of law and so sail the enterprise. Rough skies persist over legalized abortion, but the girl can't help it.

Big business is built on the backs of oil businesses and electric companies. Before factories were mechanized, handfuls of craftsmen cranked out a limited number of items with pedal gears and hand tools for closed markets. The biggest business then was imperial colonization. Eventually, railroads joined the ranks of transportation under steam power, and the sea-faring empires entered the age of continental hauling. Mass transit became available, and soon thereafter, the business class began to boost imperial interests accordingly. Businesses thrived as friends of the empire, and governments were lifted high on the rising tides.

Suddenly, assembly lines hit the stock markets, and big business got rolling. The post office and then the telephone companies were joined by the light bulb and the internal combustion engine to see business reach new heights as airplanes were taking to the skies. Radio, and later television, revolutionized product advertising and the consumer base alike. Man stepped on the moon, and amusement parks joined the coliseums. Wartime spending boosted technology in spurts.

Multinational corporations emerged in force as computers and then cellular phones were invented. Internet connectivity, satellite networks, and wireless access rocketed business to every corner of the globe. The world holds its breath as alternative energy golden eggs begin to hatch. Today, small businesses outsource to bigger businesses, in the shadows of discount superstores, and rising corporate tides not only threaten to sink mom-and-pop stores but also hint at political authority as well. Learning-market consumers take hard times and market surveys in stride, but take pause when sweatshop labor creeps into precious job markets. Responsive customer service, bolstered by Better Business Bureau practices, has, so far, made up for many sins.

Slavery is a burden that is falling to the machines. There is a long way to go, but the revolution has begun. Homelessness, however, has captured the essence of subjugation in a handout. The automation of mechanization will make us all homeless in due time, and the mainstream population will be out of work. Today, we call it welfare. Tomorrow, it will be full-blown socialism. Capitalism will be left to the professionals. Workforces will be put on permanent vacations. Menial labor will be self-contained.

Long before homelessness makes slaves of us all, we will have retreated to our own haunts. There are still arts and sciences, sports and leisure, profession and philanthropy, church and state. Committed to individual paces, die hard motivation will be left to heroes and villains, achievement and discovery, power and glory. Some will have little time left for a personal life, as fringe deadlines and competition nip at unbridled dynamos' heels. Meanwhile, kindred welfare queens, homeless socialites, and trust fund playboys will run in the same mainstream circles. Space-age exploration will open up new frontiers.

Frontiers may come in droves one day. Intergalactic

exploration, like most fantasies today, is only a breakthrough away. Menial labor would be plentiful on upstart worlds. The future colonists will need to be wary of miserly proprietors on backwater worlds, who will be looking to trade in cheap labor. Slavery on new worlds could be the answer to costly overhead for many unscrupulous investors, who will be beyond the reach of imperial officials. Full-blown human trafficking is always a threat in frontier lands. On the other hand, an entire race in bondage is the scope of an empire. Very little is worse than a land of slavers, lurking across a sea.

6

OLD BUSINESS

Everyone hopes and dreams that the diplomatic corps can resolve any and all sources of friction and conflict in the world. A fine system of embassies is the pinnacle of global harmony for any state department. Appointed ambassadors, diplomatic attachés, and covert operatives adhere to standards set by heads of state. These outposts, on home soil in foreign cities, are the destination for any national citizen caught behind the wrong lines.

When diplomacy fails, they send in the marines first. Spearhead storm troopers take beachheads using hovercraft landings, jarhead commandos, and satellite intelligence reports. Tactical personnel with expert panache secure facilities with crisp protocols and fast reflexes.

Armies lend multifaceted support and build on the foundations provided by advance assault forces, eventually accomplishing great objectives with their massive numbers, crack engineering skills, and mechanized and air cavalries.

Air superiority has controlled the battlefield since the early days of archers, balloons, and biplanes. The air force is the service called in to maintain battlefield support and carry out peacekeeping missions. Their mission continues into space with the pioneering astronaut program.

Control of the seas is the navy's duty. Shock and awe are a battle group's duties. These groups are led by bristling aircraft carriers, which are capable of reaching far inland with their high-tech weaponry, aircraft, and marines, doing so in a new online and cohesive battlefield. These amazing vessels are supported themselves by an array of craft, ranging from submarines to cruisers to destroyers. The new name spoken is on the high seas is stealth. From camouflaged frogmen to top secret ship designs, matte strokes makeover classic borders to evade enemy detection grids and live fire.

The National Guard is also part of the armed forces, but it is not slated for foreign service. Their units across the country primarily maintain home presence and answer federal emergencies as required. They also answer to the commander in chief and the chain of command. The secretary of defense takes orders from the president and relays them to the global combatant commanders, who oversee all armed forces in their regions. Generals command battalions, and admirals command battle groups. Commanding officers rank as colonels and majors, or captains and commanders in the navy, then execute missions based on the talents of navy lieutenant commanders and captains in the rest, lieutenants, and specialist warrant officers, plus the blood of enlisted men. Then there is the Coast Guard, which is on duty day and night saving lives, protecting borders, and answering to the Department of Homeland Security since shortly after the September 11 tragedy.

When all has gone to hell, the people themselves organize and fight back. Spy networks born from smaller resistance cells begin to organize and get down to business. These freedom fighters, born of good intentions, eventually evolve into ferocious fighters and vicious companions. These troops will live off the land and billet in family residences as guerrilla fighters. While these units can seem glamorous in print, the dreary existence they lead in the quest for justice and recognition, more often than not leads to war crimes, followed by terrorist labels, dissension and attrition in the ranks as drawn out stalemates set in. Liable to take off without notice, or worse, sell out without notice, these cold and desperate folks can lose themselves and then their discipline. These miserable conditions show the personal horrors of war beyond ashes and rubble. Refugees become targets, girls become sex crimes, and weapons replace wallets. Ragtag organization and poor solidarity between wanted leaders and maverick lieutenants leave idealistic followers to their own disillusioned devices, between persecution and atrocity.

Meanwhile, Mommy's little angel hits the streets, attempting to comprehend a crumbling world and, more importantly, a crumbling personal life. The kid brother emerges from a youth group, or other gainful affiliation, into a youth culture impossibly removed from his own sensibilities. His distressed realizations herald salacious revelations starting at home. Cagey sisters and a strapped mother neglect him and keep secrets as their prerogative. Rude brothers over an absent father throw verbal abuse and domestic work into the cauldron, keeping the young hero busy and oblivious. Alas, the little prince is left to fend for himself, lost in a world of reindeer games that knows his privileged family and their sins better than he does.

Out on the hard streets, twisted sisters have sexual relations in a rebellious and profitable fashion. She learned this behavior from her drug addicted but doting mother, who routinely makes ends meet herself, with a little discreet prostitution to make amends for poor provider choices. His angry dad storming off, but not before doling out some liberal smacks, is dim in his memory. His bullying brothers grow up to be absent dads, to be found across town, involved in crime and decadence.

Finally on the streets himself, the good little boy begins to get acquainted with charmed friends and mutual neighbors, accepting a bigger war effort picture that the rest of the family has known.

Stalked by furtive whispers, polite deference, and wing-man cold shoulder, however, soon gives way to the stiff wartime truth of the matter, and the little prince wakes to a new colder, harder day and even harder choices on 'El Camino' in a beast master family of party girls, common hoods, and degenerate, evil empire honors, courtesy of a bittersweet, war machine economy.

Still seeking to keep all his ducks in a row, he turns to church resources, to find the Power and Glory he has taken for granted for so long. A kindly priest, or someone of similar stature, takes the time to clue the boy into some facts of life and illuminates his uncultivated mind. The world of mixed company does indeed start with the Power and the Glory. It is in mixed company that the man is king of his castle, the woman is affectionate and devoted, and the devil is epitomized by the evils of human trafficking. His religion is one of disciples not slaves. The boy is taught that girls mature faster than boys, but to correct wayward women in his life with scripture not bitch slapping, and to stand up to scoundrel men with calm demeanor and time-honored Christian gender roles.

Alas, a new World Wide Web has dawned on the Power and the Glory, and they have taken pornography to new levels of chauvinism, with theatrical expansion, while sanctimonious cowboys, still bucking the world's oldest profession, are stripped of their guns. Curiously, cases of enchanting princes coming up bullfrog street-kings, upon true love's magic kiss, get dismissed as headfuls of bad wiring. They may not be the stars, but like the comic relief in a movie, they know the score.

Feminine sanctimony, meanwhile, spirals further off the natural order as in vitro fertilization pregnancy joins abortion on the flip-side, expanding her potential in lifestyle options even further. Barroom politics has come a long way since the days of betrothal and dowry benchmarks. To give context to the world that gave rise to the politics of men, a few lamentable tales will follow concerning modern historic roots, urban legends, and psychotic secrets.

First, sightings of trouble, deep in the woods claimed the Power and the Glory were found living the lives of satyrs, attended to by a bevy of sexy woodland nymphs. A lifestyle tainted by magic but seductive nonetheless. Demonized in children bedtime stories, these sensual creatures can still be spotted today in any given urban jungle, if you know where to look.

In modern urban legends, we hear about ornery backwoods hay seeds that liven things up by abducting wayward travelers or pain-in-the-neck pop ins for a season or two of ribald deviltry and chilling serial crime indulgences. Upwardly mobile kissing cousins host swanky Halloween parties to welcome cuckold newcomers to swinger neighborhoods and family deflowering showers.

The Mexican whore built for charity may be young and pretty for a wandering band of outlaws, but eventually she grows large and old. A working girl by demand for many years, with plenty of work left over for growing offspring. Strung out and at the end of her rope, she gives up her only piece—a rusty old Swiss Army knife, and last gasp to ask her gawky son to carve a piece out of a man that may or may not be his dad in a win-win gamble for Mommy and the girls, maybe in the long run, and the possible birth of a surprise Swiss army in the barrio..

Meanwhile, long after the abolishment of slavery, deep in the inner city, the sisters have their own problems, juggling gangbangers and baby daddies. As it is all over the world, hard up girls are trolled by local school dances and annual graduation parties as early as grade school. Junkie moms sell less fortunate ones' virtues for an evening's fix, or until child welfare can catch up to her.

Not to be outdone by the formidable past. America the beautiful - girl on the street circled the old west cathouse wagons in Las Vegas, Nevada, and hunkered down with big casino money and consummate entertainers. Meanwhile, many of her old-world sisters still languish around the globe as second-class citizens.

Today's shrinking middle class enjoys a hedonistic divorce rate among civil union and hardcore background. The broken home sees one-bedroom apartments married to alimony checks, child support delinquents skipping out on struggling single-mom households, and damaged goods club resurgences.

Only children pose dysfunctions all their own. All boy broods show problems in single family home housekeeping. All girl families circle the afghans and practice gargoyle faces in the mirror. Mixed gender troops share crossover interests and scatter away, left to their own devices. Step siblings can show racial disharmony as well as clashing styles or even thorny mutual attraction. Generation gaps bulge out in large families, while small families are left to stand back to back.

The migrained wings of liberty are a hard lesson for some; for others, however, not so much. Before you dip the tips of yours in blood, pay heed to the anatomy of the wings. On the right side is the conservative, on the left is the liberal, and somewhere toward the middle is the crease where you live out your existence.

Wings of liberty are parceled out by the lands we live in. We beat our wings to the letter of the law; we elect our officials by the color of our feathers. We hold the body in judgment by clown-college rote.

Extremists, beware that you don't stray too far from the meaty and stable body of the people. A crease established too far out on the wings, will find a no-fly zone of intolerance and bigotry— badlands that only a matrix of conservative scorpions and liberal snakes survive. Nice guys finish last, but yours will be the one wing dipped in blood if you stray too far from hand holding, neighborhood norms.

On the conservative wing, you'll find the chessmen to be tycoons—the captains of industry and the corporate structures. Also the puritanical consisting mostly of religious communities and secular philanthropies. Militants, both active and proactive, round out the house for the right engine's components, mounted where the devil makes you do it, when opposites attack.

On the liberal wing, opposites attract the same lifestyle opportunities seen on the conservative wing, if not the same choices. The chessmen here are found in a welfare system that is a civil juggernaut, as big a pacifier as anything the military uses.

Also, the girls are sinners under the table, and so are the boys.

Barley phased black market dealers already look for greener

pastures as marijuana circles back again, this time catching up with

civilization as it approaches self-medicating speeds. This left wing

engine is very human; it is evenly matched for the right, sharing

the color of money—but the housing always wins. Black or white,

each piece is a legitimate token in play.

7

VITAL POWERS

This quick reference guide of government obligation to the people is a simple tool that builds on what we have by using the wisdom we have gained. To rise from the post-apocalyptic ashes of ruin, as epic holocaust survivors come together to rebuild lost empires without missing the beat—or for colonies looking to rebuild that old new-world feel in an off-world community.

The Sovereign Judges of Jurispublic Rule

The Lord Marshal is the commander in chief and patrolling jurisdiction needed to safeguard his civilian constituency with whatever available resources are ready. He is a sitting judge, in charge of modern police and military protection for his own great race. He relies on counsel from the Attorney General, who is the successor to his bench. His appointment by the boss general, who is his compatriot by ethnicity, is the inception of the state.

The Boss General is the chief executive officer. He works hard to rebuild civilian communities with the resources afforded to his people. He is a sitting judge. His jurisdiction is to regulate businesses of every kind, out to the arts and sciences, across products and services, from marketing and exploration to payroll and financing. His motto is "Spectator Sports since Day One." If there is a cry of no confidence, or if he abdicates, his successor will be elected by his peers. The Treasury Director succeeds his bench after his death, followed by the Finance Director if necessary. The new Boss General is free to appoint new blood to the benches he answers for at the beginning of his rule, or he may choose to stay the course as he sees fit. He is an ethnic compatriot of his constituents classified Asian, Caucasian, Latino, Mediterranean, Middle Eastern, Negro, Polynesian, or Native American.

The State Commissioner is the head of state. He shores up nose-diving problem areas with human resources, guild policies, and a bill of rights. He is a sitting judge and the Director of Welfare and State, with municipalities, counties, and constituencies under his jurisdiction, as well as foreign diplomacy dibs or delegation as the need arises. He safeguards his old world constituents from sanctimonious, frontier prejudice and breaks fatal cycles born from cultural deprivation. He is appointed by the Boss General, who is his compatriot by ethnicity. The Scout Director succeeds him.

The Union Pope is the head of Western Catholicism, appointed by the church, and the wielder of the 666 card in a fledgling world. A holy trump card, the 666 card is a veto that mans up to call a spade a spade. He is the keeper of the Holy Encyclopedia of Gabriel – Old Pantheon (world religions before Christ) and New Pantheon (world religions after Christ), with its accompanying yearly almanacs, comprised of all eight ethnic churches' letters to the pope about the holy seal of authenticity coming out of his papal district. This tribal chief is also a lone government official worthy of mention, but he is not a Sovereign Judge. He is the ambassador to all the denominations in the union of all the Jurisdictions that rise. He oversees dioceses and parishes, as well as the layman's halls of power, with Holy Bible in hand.

To protect, and to serve...

The sheriff is the most fundamental element of all in an enlightened culture. This elected official keeps the peace in the way the constituents see fit. The sheriff's office is the hub for all public notices and license registrations. The sheriff patrols beats, maintains a capable constabulary, and protects the wings of liberty. The office is in the middle of three overlapping jurisdictions, falling between municipal police and jurispublic rangers. Union troopers operate at the federal level.

The marshal is the most fundamental element in a radical culture. The marshal is an official who is appointed by the boss general to keep the peace in the way the establishment sees fit. This office is the hub meant to support neighborhood watch needs. The office also oversees safe treatment of prisoners of the state.

The powers that be...

Cabinets are the headquarters for the administrative bodies that delegate authority to subsequent bureaucracies from higher powers. These bodies address the elements a culture deems vital for its survival. Directors, previously known as secretaries or ministers, are all appointed by the State Commissioner; they oversee the particular divisions under their auspices, promoting healthy growth and responsible practices. All executive business is tended to by the board of directors of the jurispublic or the United Jurispublics. The logistics director is the chairman of this board.

The Treasury Director is the guardian of the state's bank reserves. He is the custodian of historical documents and other national treasures. His federal repository mints coins, prints currency and bank checks, and provides safety deposit boxes for official use. It is the destination for all manner of taxes. He prints only as much money as the treasury collateral allows.

The Finance Director is responsible for smart investments, profitable returns, and is in charge of promoting jurispublic business. His office oversees government bonds, commodities, collateral, and offers industrial incentives, as well as ensuring fair savings and loan practices with checking accounts and bank card credit lines and sound investment opportunities.

The Logistics Director facilitates the delivery of products and materials bound for the community or export and oversees Custom's inspections of imports. He ensures safe products, fresh perishables, and quality edibles in the stores. He meets crises with limited supplies and monies bound for vital markets, key merchants, and trade export.

The Attorney General is the lawyer that advocates for the interests of all three benches. The Attorney General submits an opinion to the benches on each docket matter in accordance with enlightened and humane thinking, allowing for informed views on pending business. Also working for the public at large, the Attorney General streamlines government bureaucracy with legal disclosures and public client services. He is the Boss General's legal presence; he advises the Lord Marshal's on tactical activities and the State Commissioner on mainstream relief efforts with attorney-client privilege.

The Surgeon General is the cavalry for the constituency at large. This person is a medical practitioner of mind and body and the cultivator and manufacturer of reliable pharmaceutical and recreational drugs. He also ferments, brews, and distills alcohols. He is the keeper of the reference library that is dedicated to supporting an antiseptic culture. He cultivates deprived minds in art, music, and literature, in keeping with his traditional passions. His sworn priorities are inpatient hospitals and outpatient clinics to dispense professional aid.

The Postmaster General is in charge of the lines of communication and the mail. This person is equipped to collect and distribute correspondence, parcels, and freight in communities struggling to maintain cultural ties and establish relations with communities outside of their own. The postmaster is responsible for mail carriers, and efficient post offices that provide post office boxes, business windows, and bulletin boards for public notices and warrants. This office is also tasked with the establishment and upkeep of official cellular towers and Internet capabilities, where possible.

The Textiles Director is the hero of the fashion industry and beyond. He is also the provider of skins and furs, as well as other natural and synthetic fibers, in keeping with modern cultural standards and environmental needs.

The Farming Director is responsible for providing sufficient crop yields to nourish jurispublic man, beast, cash crop opportunities. This person's mission is to produce safe and regular consignments for commercial delivery.

The Ranching Director is the producer of both meat and dairy products to satisfy the dietary and commercial needs of the community. He ensures the production of quality food products and industrial materials.

The Mechanics Director is mobile, skilled labor and resourceful, site engineer, serving dependent commuters and demanding end users with safe products, services, and training materials. He maintains an equipped garage for tuning up, servicing, refueling, and resupplying of required jurispublic fleets. He maintains a salvage yard as well as a work shed and, if applicable, a shipyard and a port. This office oversees private sector patents, public utilities, and customer service needs.

The Mining Director is the producer of sufficient fuels and minerals for health and prosperity. Specifically, he wants to satisfy the mineral needs of medical and scientific laboratories as well as the commercial and dietary needs of the jurispublic. He also must meet any industrial needs for mined raw materials. He considers the strategic value of each mine and its long-term contributions to the community.

The Fishing, Hunting, Logging, or Salvage Director performs from one, up to all of these four function under one roof, adopting the appropriate titles. This person maintains the appropriate equipment for the tasks at hand and is expected to oversee responsible subsistence from natural ecosystems.

The Professions Director is a renaissance man of science. This office provides licenses for white-collar professionals. The Professions Director is also the headmaster and school teacher, if necessary, for eligible students according to progressive curriculum and literacy emergency. This office also oversees museums, wildlife refuges, and regional ecologies through a growing system of Pax University resources.

The Publishing Director is the operator of the printing press and online feeds. This person is responsible for modern newspaper sections and headlines in daily news, monthly and quarterly publications, maps, calendars, almanacs, reference materials, and contemporary literary works.

The Arts Director is the custodian of precious self-expression and priceless masterpieces in the making. He maintains a dynamic program of groomed constituents who are self-motivated and proficient in their mediums. He sponsors musical and literary works, arts and crafts, performance academies and prototypes.

The Entertainment Director is the emcee of the jurispublic. He is responsible for theater, cinema, broadcasting, and gaming. All works on stage and screen are available to him in the pursuit of quality diversions. He is responsible for artistic integrity, popular genres, professional products, contemporary broadcasts, and audience satisfaction.

The Athletics Director coordinates the athletic programs for the jurispublic. He oversees sporting events and sports teams from the recreational to the professional levels. He ensures the health and fitness of all participants by adhering to standardized fitness and performance tests. He also trains the community in self-defense and first aid.

The Security Director is the gateway to military service. He offers enlistment opportunities for all the branches of service, as well as career planning services and state education. His services are available to local and private groups, in addition to the military, in support of well conceived law enforcement, properly trained peacekeeping troops, and well-coordinated police activity.

The Concierge Director is the administrator of vice and virtue in the jurispublic. He is positioned to respond to individual needs and situations with efficient network policies, safe elements, generous selections, and strict guidelines. He hosts a behaved clientele, and he coordinates the pursuit of quality leisure, bountiful luxury, scintillating companionship, adventurous spirit, and market value.

The Mastermind Director is the professional authority that sponsors extraordinary activities behind closed doors. He is the patron of blood sports and dens of vice. He answers to the marshal's office and the sitting benches in criminal and taxable matters. The mastermind has deputy-marshal powers in his toolbox, as he is officially the smartest man in the room. His purpose is to ensure legitimate participation and humane treatment.

The Scout Director is the scoutmaster for children and seniors women and men in a socialist culture. His statistics monitor progress, advance prodigy, target well-rounded objectives, and bear down on remedial deficiencies. He counsels arrested development on courteous respect, valiant hearts, just rewards and first class scouting. Working in tandem with other officials, he operates a balanced work-study program focused on diligence, individual excellence, well-rounded education, and existential merit-badge advancement.

Merchants operate and pay taxes licensed and zoned under commercial regulations. These various community members cooperate to bring products and services to market, improve infrastructure as needed and permitted, and comply with Chamber of Commerce dues, policies, and crisis alerts.

The Star Chamber Lodge is a fraternal order with a ladies' auxiliary. It is open to all upstanding men, as well as their wives and children. Members pay dues, respect bylaws, and annually elect officers for president, vice president, financial secretary, treasurer, secretary, warden, ritual chancellor, inside guard, outside guard, and four color guard positions. They annually elect one of three trustees for a three-year term. The chaplain and the youth director are appointed annually. Annual ladies' auxiliary elections install a president, vice president, treasurer, and secretary. New chapters and country club annexes are voted on annually as well. Member activities include mixers, league sports teams, homeless charity drives, and parade details. There is co-op credit union banking with mortgage, scholarship and insurance incentives, aiming to help keep lodge image steady. Membership in a hooded fellowship bonds men by blood oath, key club, and renaissance endeavor. All members are available and eligible to conduct business in one cultivated good faith business network with fair price and quality service.

A judge is a regulating element in cultural turmoil. This elected official wields the scales of justice with responsible poise and repetitive composure. He presides over the court before defendant and plaintiff, with jury, court stenographer, bailiff and gallery in attendance.

A lawyer is a private advocate available to represent individuals in death and tax matters, civil and criminal disputes, and business and household counsel in accordance with enlightened jurisprudence.

A juror is a layperson who is brought into a trial to sound off on the matters at hand in a twelve-person group. Disputes resolved in this manner require a unanimous vote from the jury. A trial then goes back to the court's officers for a closing verdict and sentencing as applicable.

A witness saw the events under scrutiny by officers of the court. It is a force wielded by swift justice, along with hard evidence and police records to reach a fair resolution.

A plaintiff is the injured party in a dispute, who is seeking legal recourse. The plaintiff is free to use a lawyer, as recommended and encouraged by enlightened courtroom procedures.

A defendant is the accused party in a dispute, needing to render civil answers to actions deemed malicious, callous, and or unsound. The defense strategy must be in accordance with enlightened powers and privileges bestowed upon citizens as civil rights. No one in the jurispublic is beyond a court summons. Everyone needs due representation; it must be available to the accused upon request.

A warden is the administrative person in a correctional institution that is rehabilitating wayward hard cases according to hard-nosed cultural regulations and humane objectives. He maintains facilities for prevailing corporal punishment, capital punishment, and prison confinement. He is the benefactor of the Cradle Robbers' Farewell Hall. In the spirit of the damned and family, friends or town folk as determined reasonable by judicial decree during sentencing, and the final wishes of the lawyered up convict.

Senates are a big deal for growing constituencies letting their voices be heard in ancient town hall surroundings. State department affairs also manifest, embassies are established by a global community, and golden ages are in ascendance. A senator's purpose is to maintain order through elected representation over sprawling cultural, commercial, and industrial affairs. A senator remembers that worship is spoken for by precious blood, sacred heart, and divine specimen as well as a crocodile tears compass.

The County Union has three houses: the Charter House is responsible for serving the land, the Funnel House is responsible for serving the people, and the Commercial Senate is responsible for serving businesses. To become law, each house's legislation must pass through the other houses and be approved by each sovereign judge as well as by the union pope. Each county in the jurispublic sends one representative to each congressional house.

The mayors mind the store at the local level, employing the same methodology in a panel consisting of the town boss, the town marshal, and the town commissioner and in the administrative bodies behind them, including the town doctor, the town attorney, and the town postmaster.

The Sovereign Judges exist at the state and federal levels. A federal Boss General is elected from any of the sitting judges with the proper qualifications, leaving an open bench for his home jurispublic to fill. He is subject to calls of no confidence but may also serve a life term. If he chooses to abdicate at any point, the federal bench is once again open to election. A jurispublic can lose a panel of benches and a board of directors in one election if the new Boss General chooses to appoint his own dream team alongside him. The panel sits as a whole to rule on cases as they see fit and for the cabinet as resources and guides.

If the Treasury Director is unable to become the Boss General, the Finance Director assumes the position in the interim. An election is then required, for which the Finance Director is eligible. Popular crown princes may be appointed as successor directors, same as anyone, with the blessing of the State Commissioner. They must meet required credentials before becoming eligible. The Lord Marshal and the Attorney General are licensed attorneys. The Boss General, the Treasury Director, and the Finance Director are business executives. And the State Commissioner and the Scout Director are military veterans.

The judges are guards. They serve the people with one eye on the benches and the other on the community's goals. They make

decisions according to judicial precedence and enlightened vision.

The dons are enlightened members of the community who wish

to participate in political activity in an influential manner. They

serve the people according to their abilities.

The citizens are volunteers in the community who wish to

participate in all manner of activities and in the development of

something greater. They serve at large.

The subjects are consumers in the community who wish to

participate in matters of fellowship and family and want to see

children exceed their parents.

The peasants do not wish to participate in the community. They

desire to subsist on their own merits and are left to do so in

accordance with jurispublic edicts.

The slaves are community members that have fallen from grace, whether by convicted criminal activity or civil delinquency. They are in the service of the State Commissioner and serve according to labor needs and any specialized skills they have in exchange for reduced sentences and debts. They are the abject bottom of Jurispublic society, fully under the protection of the Marshal.

These new halls of power should serve well in preserving desirable melting-pot variety or cannibalize on the fly for next level super power thinking or an endangered species's immediate needs.

The Federalist Grand Party is the platform of the welfare state. The Federalist State Commissioner stands for human interests, the Democratic Boss General stands for business interests, and the Republican Lord Marshal stands for national interests. The sitting benches preside over each house.

8

EARTH

Hell is a frumpy seventh heaven back booth, watching the dream life from across the room. Hell is an embroiled crazy eight deserter, all dressed up with nowhere to go, stranded between a misty seventh heaven and a cloud nine fog. Hell is a gallant cloud nine round table, on borrowed time because of spiraling crazy eight destiny. Hell is a skeptical perfect-ten death wish. A supreme hard body and a creature of taste that is worth their weight in gold, livid and tearing into cloud nine deadbeats. Hell is the lone, eleventh hour gunshot ringing out into the house, that is heard deep in the heart of Texas.

Purgatory is that place between good intentions and catastrophic failure, where big-city lights continue to sweep for any more signs of criminal activity. It is where blood, sweat, and tears have immediate meaning and integrity is on the line. By test of virtue and vice, young punks face the music from all sides. The drag net is in effect, and Texas Instruments are all business. All points bulletins are looking for Butterfingers, and old man Louisville commits his Monster Mash to memory, because the missing link just shot everyone's all-American. There's a cry to dissolve the unholy union. Martial disciplines and positive mental attitude are your only friends. Spoils of war are the only trophies that will set you free, since heaven doesn't want you, hell is afraid you'll take over and clown college was seventh heaven through perfect ten. Butterfingers will have left an alibi for all scramblers, but the last thing you remember before coming to in front of the police is the doctor saying, "This won't hurt a bit."

Heaven is everlasting bliss. Everything is perfect; the muscle car is still a priceless treasure.. The sun has long since extinguished, but throngs of humans still live on, off world. Bad words have no meaning left because the argument is over. All dogs get to heaven –and there are two cherished girls for every boy. The Boss General offers endless time-sharing vacation homes on exotic planets. Psychic haunts are the home of precision sciences and awakening humanity. And Daddy is perfect, and Mommy is perfect, and the kids are perfect, and friends and family are perfect. Everyone sleeps soundly in the beds they have made for themselves. The concierge has all the right treats at the gate. A golden-age father knows there are worse devils in heaven than his princes. A son never forgets that coming down hard is just like getting back to nature. And all is well in the kindred worlds of a fabled land called Texmania.

Vayan con Dios.

9

SPACE

In 1969 man walked on the moon for the first time. Neal
Armstrong's Apollo footprint culminated the early space race. The
Soviet Union's Sputnik program and the United States' Mercury
program, eventually rose from the cold war to realize an orbital
bonanza. The space shuttle reusable reentry vehicle experiment
was a dramatic success with its hefty cargo bay lugging impressive
loads and precision technology into position, including powerful
telescopes, and international space station modules. On other
fronts GPS satellite technology, launched on independent vehicles,
joins communication, environmental, and surveillance satellites in
consolidating planet unity. The rocket is still a risky proposition,
however, as are reentry vehicles. Costly accidents have claimed
precious payloads and heroic lives.

Probes and rovers do the hands on exploration these days. All
planets have been visited. Mars is an object of scrutiny in the

search for extra terrestrial life. Liquid water, harboring microbial life is the grail sought there. Planetary moons have been visited as well. Jupiter's Europa flirts at a liquid sea, also a possible refuge for life beneath its ice. Saturn's moon Titan most notably, actually being entered by a probe to see methane rivers and rocky mountains under its cloud-filled sky. Intelligent extraterrestrial life, meanwhile, is being hunted in the stars. Radio astronomy opens up not only visible line of sight to study, but transmissions as well. Detecting precursor civilizations is a long shot, nevertheless, Search for Extra Terrestrial Intelligence (SETI) is the line our conspiracy theory culture dangles on.

Several nations sport space programs in the twenty first century with lofty missions all their own. Private sector space ventures look to improve upon margin benchmarks in safety and profit. The space elevator, is the new golden goose on the drawing table. Mothballed until the ribbon technology is perfected, it finds itself alongside the new crew exploration vehicle Orion. The Orion is the sole survivor of the Constellation program, chartered to return to the moon, and then on to Mars, before being canceled for budgetary reasons. Heavily influence by Apollo precedents, it steps back from ultimately shaky, shuttle technology to get the job done. Capital ships in space are still a dream for now. The realization of the space elevator would change that. The ribbonroad to space is the safety precaution commuters can put their faith in. For still being hobbled by interstellar distances, however, the solar system offers plenty of interplanetary consolation to its tenants. A speck in the universe, Sol is still home.

ABOUT THE AUTHOR

Gabriel Othon is a graduate of the University of Illinois at Urbana-Champaign with a BA in political science. He enjoys the bounty of modern civilization and hopes to see it go the distance. He lives in Downers Grove, Illinois, with his twin brother.

www.ingramcontent.com/pod-product-compliance
Lightning Source LLC
Chambersburg PA
CBHW072317290526
45794CB00002B/688